Tea Cakes & Tarts

get started
making

Tea Cakes & Tarts

step-by-step recipes
for tempting teatime treats

Yamashita Masataka

Marshall Cavendish
Cuisine

Chef Yamashita Masataka was trained in Tsuji Culinary Institute, a well-known and respected culinary institute in Osaka, Japan. He worked at various pâtisseries around Japan before starting his own pâtisserie in Nara.

The pâtisserie quickly became one of the top in Nara. Eight years later, yearning for new challenges and a change of scenery, chef Yamashita moved to Singapore where he took charge of the kitchen at Pâtisserie Glacé, turning it into a haven for delightful cakes and pastries. Chef Yamashita soon saw an opportunity to revive his pâtisserie from Japan and re-established Flor Pâtisserie.

Today, chef Yamashita no longer runs Flor, but his own Japanese artisan pâtisserie at Tanjong Pagar Plaza, aptly named Chef Yamashita.

The recipes in this book were taken from chef Yamashita's first cookbook, *Tanoshii*, which clinched the Best First Cookbook award at the Gourmand World Cookbook Awards 2013.

www.chefyamashita.com
www.facebook.com/chefyamashita

Dedication

To my parents, who did not approve
of my decision to become a pastry chef
in the beginning, but who grew to see my passion
in it and have been supporting me
in every possible way ever since.

To my wife and best friend, Ami Yamashita,
for always being by my side with a smile.
She is the only person who truly understands me
and knows exactly what to say when
the going gets tough.

Contents

Introduction

First of all, I would like to thank you for your support in buying my cookbook. Let me start by sharing with you briefly about how I became a pastry chef. I was born in Nara, Japan, and from a young age, I have always loved baking. I enjoyed making beautiful cakes, sweets and pastries for my family and friends, and I found great satisfaction in knowing that a simple but well-made cake could bring so much joy and laughter to my loved ones.

Many of my peers chose to become lawyers and doctors, but I knew my heart was and will always belong in the kitchen, so I chose the unconventional route. It was not easy in the beginning, but through hard work and determination, I rose to become the executive pastry chef of the world famous Schlossgasse Mozart in Okayama, Japan. That was when I decided it was time for a new challenge and I opened Flor Patisserie in Nara, Japan.

Over the years, many of my loyal customers have asked why I did not have a cookbook to my name. The truth is I have always felt it was not the right time for me to write a cookbook as I have so much more to learn—a chef never stops learning! So it was a very humbling experience to have so many supporters request that I write a cookbook.

When I started working on this cookbook, my main challenge was picking which of my best-loved recipes to showcase, as it was my desire to share all my knowledge through this book. After all these months of hard work, with the support of my very understanding team, I have to say I am completely satisfied with this book that you now hold in your hands.

The reason why I decided to write this cookbook was simple. Through the years, many loyal customers have also asked me why baking cakes is so difficult and why their cakes always fail. I strongly believe that this need not be so! Baking should not be hard or stressful, but fun and enjoyable!

So, in a way, this cookbook is the expression of my appreciation to all my loyal customers for their continuous support through the years, and my answer to all these questions on baking. It is also a profession of my personal belief that making cakes, sweets and pastries is for everyone, from the novice home baker to the most experienced baker.

I trust there is something in this cookbook for everyone. I have included step-by-step photographs with easy-to-follow instructions for each recipe as, to me, baking is very visual, so by showing each step, it's like having me in your kitchen, beside you, guiding you every step of the way. You won't need fanciful equipment or expensive ovens to bake a good cake, just the right attitude and passion to bake.

Lastly, I will like to emphasise that baking is all about having fun in the kitchen, so don't feel demoralised when your cake fails to turn out. Instead, try again and don't give up! Remember, even the most experienced chefs may fail, but it is through failure that we come up with something even more amazing!

So do have fun trying out the various recipes in this cookbook, and remember to always enjoy the baking process. May all your cakes, sweets and pastries bring smiles and laughter to you and your loved ones!

Yamashita Masataka

PÂTE SUCRÉE

Makes 600 g dough, enough for two 18-cm tart bases

Pastry flour 200 g

Bread flour 50 g

Unsalted butter 180 g,
  at room temperature

Salt 1/2 tsp

Sugar 95 g

Vanilla extract 1/2 tsp

Egg 1, at room temperature,
  lightly beaten

Almond powder 40 g

1. Sift together pastry flour and bread flour. Set aside. In a large bowl and using a hand whisk, whisk butter, salt, sugar and vanilla extract until smooth and pale.

2. Whisk in beaten egg, half portion at a time, ensuring full incorporation after each addition. Whisk in almond powder, then flour mixture until just combined.

3. Using a rubber spatula, scrape base and sides of bowl until dry ingredients are no longer visible, taking care not to over mix.

4. Place dough on a sheet of plastic wrap and cover tightly. Dough needs to be refrigerated overnight before using.

TIP

If you are preparing this dough ahead of time, you will still need to refrigerate it overnight before placing it into the freezer for storing. This dough can be kept frozen for up to 1 month.

To prevent over mixing, be sure to use a rubber spatula to incorporate the flours and stop as soon as the flours are no longer visible.

Basic
Recipe

ROLL SPONGE

Makes one 30-cm square sponge

—~~~~~— Ingredients ~~~~~—

Eggs 6, at room temperature

Sugar 190 g

Milk 75 g

Unsalted butter 38 g

Pastry flour 145 g, sifted

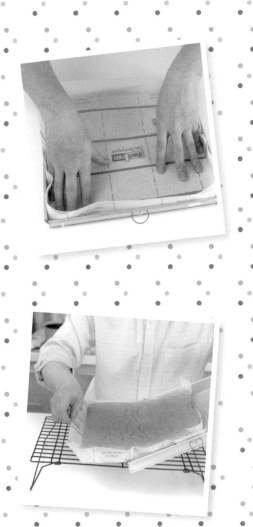

~~~~~~~~~~~~~~~~~~~~~~~~~ Method ~~~~~~~~~~~~~~~~~

1. Preheat oven to 180°C. Line a shallow 30-cm square baking tray with parchment paper, leaving a 2-cm overhang. Set aside. Fill a pot with water up to 4 cm high and simmer over medium heat.

2. In a heatproof bowl, whisk eggs and sugar lightly. Place bowl over pot of simmering water and whisk constantly in large strokes until mixture reaches 40°C. Transfer to the bowl of a stand mixer.

3. Whisk warm egg mixture at high speed until mixture doubles in volume and turns very pale. Meanwhile, in a saucepan over medium heat, heat milk and butter to 80°C and remove from heat.

4. When egg mixture is ready, turn mixer speed to low. Add warm milk and butter mixture. Beat for 5 seconds, then increase speed to high and beat until mixture is uniform.

5. Switch to using a rubber spatula and fold in sifted flour until fully incorporated. Scrape base and sides of mixing bowl thoroughly. Be careful not to over mix.

6. Pour batter into prepared baking tray. Using a flat scraper, very gently smoothen surface of batter in one direction, ensuring a uniform height, especially at the sides. Scrape away any batter clinging to the sides of the tray to prevent it from burning.

7. Bake for 10–12 minutes or until surface of sponge is brown. Test if sponge is done by pressing the centre lightly. It should spring back. Place sponge on a wire rack. Peel away paper at the side. Leave to cool for about 30 minutes.

8. To peel off parchment paper at bottom of sponge, place a cutting board over the sponge and flip it over. Peel off paper and flip sponge back upright. The roll is now ready for use.

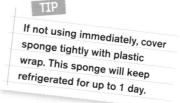

TIP

If not using immediately, cover sponge tightly with plastic wrap. This sponge will keep refrigerated for up to 1 day.

SPONGE

Makes one 21-cm round cake

~~~~~~~~~~~~~~~ Ingredients ~~~~~~~~~~~~~~~

Unsalted butter 25 g

Milk 40 g

Eggs 6, at room temperature

Sugar 170 g

Honey 16 g

Glucose 16 g

Pastry flour 170 g, sifted

1. Preheat oven to 180°C. Line a 21-cm round baking tin with parchment paper, leaving a 2-cm overhang. Simmer butter and milk until butter is melted. Remove from heat.

2. Fill a pot with water up to 4 cm high and simmer over medium heat. In a heatproof bowl, lightly whisk eggs, sugar, honey and glucose.

3. Place bowl over pot of simmering water and whisk constantly in large strokes until mixture is warm, about 40°C. Transfer to the mixing bowl of a stand mixer.

4. Using a stand mixer, whisk mixture at high speed until tripled in volume and very pale. Use the whisk to draw a ribbon in the batter. The shape should not dissolve immediately.

5. Using a spatula, fold in flour, a third at a time, ensuring full incorporation after each addition. Turn the bowl as you fold the flour in, and scrape base and sides of bowl well.

6. Using a rubber spatula and mixing in a circular motion, mix in warm milk and butter mixture. Mix thoroughly, scraping base and sides of bowl. Stop as soon as mixture is even. Be careful not to over mix or batter will deflate, resulting in a stiff sponge.

7. Pour batter into prepared baking tin and bake for 35–40 minutes, until top of cake is golden brown and a skewer inserted into the centre of cake comes out clean. Alternatively, if the parchment paper shrinks away from the sides of the baking tin, the cake is done.

8. Unmould sponge and place on a wire rack to cool for about 30 minutes before peeling off parchment paper. Sponge is now ready for use.

CHOCOLATE GÂTEAU

Makes one 15-cm round cake

~~~~~ Ingredients ~~~~~

**Dark chocolate buttons
(58% cocoa)** 100 g

Unsalted butter 100 g,
at room temperature

Eggs 3, yolks and whites
separated

Sugar 100 g

Pastry flour 55 g, sifted

Icing sugar for dusting

1. Preheat oven to 200°C. Line a 15-cm round baking tin with parchment paper, leaving a 2-cm overhang. Fill a pot with water up to 4 cm high and simmer over medium heat.

2. Melt chocolate and butter in a heatproof bowl placed over simmering water. Stir until well mixed. Remove from heat. Add egg yolks one at a time, whisking constantly. Set aside.

3. Prepare meringue. Using a handheld mixer, whisk together egg whites and sugar at high speed until soft peaks form.

4. Using a rubber spatula, fold one-third of meringue into chocolate mixture until fully incorporated. Fold in pastry flour and mix well.

5. Fold in remaining meringue in two additions, ensuring full incorporation after each addition. Transfer batter to prepared tin.

6. Bake for 10 minutes, then lower oven temperature to 160°C and bake for 20–25 minutes, until a skewer inserted into centre of cake comes out clean.

7. Remove from oven and leave to cool for 15 minutes. When cool enough to handle, unmould cake and peel off parchment paper.

8. Leave cake to cool completely. Dust cake with icing sugar and decorate as desired before serving. Store refrigerated for up to 2 days.

> **TIP**
>
> When adding the pastry flour, be sure to mix well to activate the gluten, which is necessary to achieve the rich and dense texture of gâteau cakes.

COCONUT GULA MELAKA MADELEINES

Makes about 18 madeleines

<div align="center">~~~~~~~~~~ Ingredients ~~~~~~~~~~</div>

Melted unsalted butter for greasing mould

Pastry flour 120 g

Baking powder 2 g

Almond powder 15 g

Cornflour 5 g

Milk powder 7 g

Desiccated coconut 35 g

Honey 17 g

Heavy cream 46 g

Salted butter 46 g

Unsalted butter 46 g

Gula melaka (palm sugar) 70 g, roughly chopped

Eggs 2, at room temperature

Egg yolks 2, at room temperature

Brown sugar 80 g

1. Preheat oven to 170°C. Lightly grease a madeleine mould with melted unsalted butter. Sift together pastry flour, baking powder, almond powder, cornflour and milk powder. Whisk in desiccated coconut. Set aside.

2. Combine honey, heavy cream, both types of butter and *gula melaka* in a saucepan over medium heat. Using a wooden spoon, stir until butter and sugar are melted and mixture reaches 80°C. Set aside.

3. Using a handheld mixer, whisk eggs, egg yolks and brown sugar at high speed for 3 minutes until mixture doubles in volume and is pale. Using a rubber spatula, fold in dry ingredients.

4. Lastly, fold in warm butter mixture. Scrape base and sides of bowl thoroughly. Pour batter into prepared mould and bake for 20–25 minutes or until top of cakes are golden brown.

5. Remove from oven. Unmould cakes and leave on a wire rack to cool before serving or storing. These cakes will keep refrigerated in an airtight container for up to 3 days.

BROWNIE

Makes one 24-cm square cake

~~~~~~~~~~~~~~~~~~ Ingredients ~~~~~~~~~~~~~~~~~~

Melted butter
for greasing mould

Unsalted butter 230 g,
at room temperature

**Dark chocolate buttons
(58% cocoa)** 113 g

Sugar 320 g

Eggs 4, at room temperature

Vanilla extract 1 tsp

Pastry flour 110 g, sifted

Walnuts 125 g, roughly
chopped

1. Preheat oven to 160°C. Lightly grease a 24-cm square baking tin with melted butter, then line base with parchment paper. Fill a pot with water up to 4 cm high and simmer over medium heat.

2. Place butter and chocolate buttons into a heatproof bowl over simmering water and stir with a rubber spatula until mixture is melted and well mixed. Remove from heat.

3. Add sugar and mix until dissolved. Add eggs, two at a time, mixing well after each addition. Stir in vanilla extract. Fold in pastry flour until flour is no longer visible. Be careful not to over mix or the cake's texture will be hard.

4. Fold in chopped walnuts and pour batter into prepared tin. Bake for 30 minutes or until a skewer inserted into the centre of cake comes out clean. Remove from oven.

5. Leave cake to cool slightly before unmoulding. Place on a wire rack to cool completely. Slice to serve. This brownie will keep refrigerated in an airtight container for up to 3 days.

HOJI-CHA
BUTTER CASTELLAS

Makes two 15-cm round cakes

～～ Ingredients ～～

Melted butter
for greasing moulds

Bread flour
for coating mould

Eggs 5, at room temperature

Sugar 200 g

Glucose 50 g

Honey 15 g

Water 10 g

Hoji-cha 12 g, blended
into a powder

Pastry flour 125 g

Unsalted butter 125 g

Icing sugar for dusting

~~~~~~~~~~~~~~~ Method ~~~~~~~~~~~~~~~

1. Preheat oven to 180°C. Lightly grease the sides of two 15-cm round baking tins with melted butter, then coat with bread flour, tapping out any excess flour. Line base of tins with 2 layers of parchment paper.

2. Fill a pot with water up to 4 cm high and simmer over medium heat. In a heatproof bowl, combine eggs and sugar. Place over simmering water and whisk until mixture reaches 45°C.

3. Remove bowl from heat. Using a handheld mixer, whisk mixture at high speed until very smooth. Test consistency by drawing a ribbon in batter. The ribbon should disappear in 1–2 seconds. Set aside.

4. In a saucepan over medium heat, stir glucose, honey and water together until even. In another saucepan, heat butter until simmering. Remove from heat. Sift together *hoji-cha* powder and flour.

5. Using a rubber spatula, fold glucose mixture into batter until combined. Fold in *hoji-cha* and flour mixture, then fold in melted butter. Scrape base and sides of bowl thoroughly. Be careful not to over mix or the cake's texture will be affected.

6. Divide batter between prepared moulds. Bake for 28–30 minutes or until cakes are golden brown and a skewer inserted into the centre of cakes comes out clean. Remove from oven.

7. Leave cakes to cool slightly before unmoulding. Place on a wire rack to cool completely. Dust with icing sugar before serving. Store in an airtight container in the refrigerator for up to 2 days.

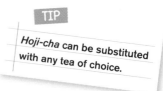

TIP

Hoji-cha can be substituted with any tea of choice.

TARTE AU FROMAGE

Makes one 18-cm round tart

Ingredients

Cream cheese 180 g,
  at room temperature

Sour cream 20 g,
  at room temperature

Egg yolks 2, at room
  temperature

Pastry flour 15 g, sifted

Lemon ½, grated for zest
  and squeezed for 10 g juice

**Round 18-cm pâte sucrée
  tart base** 1, blind-baked for
  20–25 minutes (page 14)

MERINGUE

Egg whites 40 g

Sugar 35 g

TIP

Blind-baking a tart base involves
lining the tart base with parchment
paper and filling with dried beans or
ceramic baking beans before baking
it. This pre-baked tart shell is then
ready to be used in the recipe.

Method

1. Preheat oven to 150°C. Using a handheld mixer, whisk cream cheese and sour cream at low speed until smooth. Add egg yolks and mix well.

2. Using a rubber spatula, fold flour into cream cheese mixture until flour is no longer visible. Fold in lemon zest and juice. Scrape base and sides of bowl well. Set aside.

3. Prepare meringue. Using a handheld mixer, whisk egg whites and sugar, starting at low speed and gradually increasing to high speed until mixture is white and still runny.

4. Using a rubber spatula, fold meringue, half portion at a time, into cream cheese mixture until fully incorporated. Be careful not to deflate meringue.

5. Pour mixture into partially baked tart shell and smoothen surface with an offset spatula. Bake for 20–25 minutes, or until surface starts to brown.

6. Remove from oven and leave to cool for 15 minutes. Refrigerate for at least 2 hours before slicing to serve. Store refrigerated for up to 2 days.

LA FRANCE

Makes one 18-cm round tart

~~~~~~~~~~~~~~~~~~~~~~~~~~~~~ Ingredients ~~~~~~~~~~~~~~~~~~~~~~~~~~~~~

Flour for dusting

Pâte sucrée dough
 (page 14) 300 g

Canned pear halves
 5, drained and thinly sliced
 without cutting through

CUSTARD FILLING

Eggs 3

Sugar 90 g

Heavy cream 300 g

Milk 20 g

Method

1. Dust a work surface with flour and roll dough into a 0.6-cm thick sheet. Cut out a round using a 21-cm cake ring and press into an 18-cm tart tin. Refrigerate for 30 minutes.

2. Preheat oven to 200°C. Remove tart tin from refrigerator and cover base of dough with parchment paper trimmed to size.

3. Fill tin with dried beans or pie weights and bake for 40–45 minutes, or until rim of tart shell starts to brown. Remove from oven and leave to cool. Remove parchment paper and beans or pie weights. Lower oven temperature to 160°C.

4. Prepare custard filling. In a medium bowl, lightly whisk eggs to mix. Add sugar and continue to whisk until sugar is dissolved. Add heavy cream and milk and whisk until mixture is uniform.

5. Arrange sliced pear halves in a layer on baked and cooled tart shell. Pour over custard filling and spread evenly. Bake for 35–40 minutes or until filling is set. Remove from oven.

6. Leave tart in tin and place on a wire rack to cool for 15 minutes, before refrigerating for at least 2 hours. Serve chilled. This tart can be kept refrigerated for up to 2 days.

TIP

Do not attempt to remove the tart from the tart tin while it is still hot as it may crumble. Leave the tart to cool completely before unmoulding.

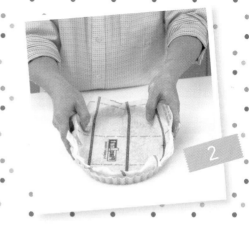

FRUIT ROLL

Makes one 30-cm long roll cake

―――― Ingredients ――――

Roll sponge (page 18)
1, chilled

Mixed diced fruit,
such as kiwi, pineapple,
strawberry, mango
and/or peach, 1 cup

Fresh fruit for decoration

Icing sugar for dusting

CHANTILLY CREAM

Heavy cream 200 g

Sugar 15 g

1. Prepare Chantilly cream. In a mixing bowl and using a handheld mixer, whisk heavy cream and sugar at high speed until soft peaks form.

2. Place sponge on a large sheet of parchment paper. Spoon three-quarters of Chantilly cream onto sponge and spread evenly using an offset spatula.

3. Top with a layer of diced fruit. Using a long knife, make a line parallel to one side of the cake, 2 cm from the edge. Use this line as the starting point to roll up the cake.

4. Roll cake up together with parchment paper, using a long ruler to keep the roll straight. Keep cake wrapped up and refrigerate for at least 30 minutes.

5. Transfer remaining Chantilly cream to a piping bag fitted with 0.8-cm round tip. Trim ends of cake, then decorate with cream and fresh fruit. Dust with icing sugar. Consume within the day.

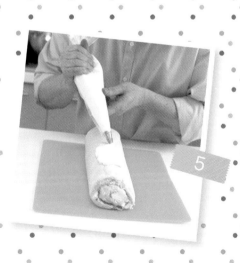

STRAWBERRY SHORTCAKE

Makes one 18-cm round cake

~~~~~~~~~~~~~~~ Ingredients ~~~~~~~~~~~~~~~

Round sponge (page 22) 1

Strawberries as needed, washed and hulled, some halved, some left whole

Icing sugar for dusting

CHANTILLY CREAM

Heavy cream 400 g

Sugar 20 g

Method

1. Cut sponge horizontally into half. Prepare Chantilly cream. In a mixing bowl and using a handheld mixer, whisk heavy cream and sugar at high speed until soft peaks form.

2. Spoon a quarter of Chantilly cream into another bowl and continue to whisk until medium soft. Spoon half the medium soft cream onto bottom half of sponge and spread evenly.

3. Arrange strawberry halves evenly over layer of cream, then spread over remaining medium soft cream. Place top half of sponge over cream and strawberry layer.

4. Using a hand whisk, whisk half the remaining soft cream until medium soft. Spoon on top of cake and use a metal spatula to spread cream over top and sides of cake.

5. Whisk remaining soft cream until medium soft. Transfer to a piping bag fitted with a 1-cm round tip. Decorate cake with cream and strawberries. Dust with icing sugar. Refrigerate for 30 minutes before serving. Consume within the day.

TIP

Do not leave whipped cream at room temperature for too long or it will melt. When not using immediately, keep it refrigerated.

SOUFFLÉ CHEESECAKE

Makes one 18-cm round cake

~~~ Ingredients ~~~

Round sponge (page 22) 1

Cream cheese 300 g,
at room temperature

Eggs 3, yolks and whites
separated

Pastry flour 24 g, sifted

Milk 75 g

Heavy cream 75 g

Lemon ½, grated for zest
and squeezed for 30 g juice

Sugar 60 g

Icing sugar for dusting

1. Preheat oven to 200°C. Line an 18-cm round baking tin with parchment paper, leaving a 2-cm overhang. Place sponge into base of baking tin. Set aside.

2. In a large bowl and using a hand whisk, whisk cream cheese until smooth. Add 2 egg yolks and whisk until incorporated, then whisk in remaining egg yolk.

3. Whisk in flour. Set aside. Bring milk and heavy cream to a simmer over low heat. Add to batter and whisk until fully incorporated. Mix in lemon zest and juice. Set aside.

4. Prepare meringue. In a large bowl and using a handheld mixer, whisk egg whites and sugar at high speed until white and still runny.

5. Fold meringue into batter half portion at a time. Pour into prepared tin and place in a deep baking tray. Fill tray with water to come 1 cm up the side of tin.

6. Bake for 15–20 minutes until the top of cake is light brown. Lower oven temperature to 160°C and continue baking for another 40–45 minutes.

7. Test if cake is done by pressing the centre of cake lightly. It should spring back. Remove baking tin from water bath and leave to cool for 5 minutes.

8. Turn cake onto a plate and peel off parchment paper. Leave to cool, then cover with a plastic container and refrigerate for 2 hours before serving.

9. Dust cake with icing sugar and decorate if desired just before serving. This soufflé can be kept refrigerated for up to 2 days.

Quantities for this book are given in Metric and American (spoon and cup) measures. Standard spoon and cup measurements used are: 1 teaspoon = 5 ml, 1 tablespoon = 15 ml and 1 cup = 250 ml. All measures are level unless otherwise stated.

LIQUID AND VOLUME MEASURES

Metric	Imperial	American
5 ml	$^1/_6$ fl oz	1 teaspoon
10 ml	$^1/_3$ fl oz	1 dessertspoon
15 ml	$^1/_2$ fl oz	1 tablespoon
60 ml	2 fl oz	$^1/_4$ cup (4 tablespoons)
85 ml	$2^1/_2$ fl oz	$^1/_3$ cup
90 ml	3 fl oz	$^3/_8$ cup (6 tablespoons)
125 ml	4 fl oz	$^1/_2$ cup
180 ml	6 fl oz	$^3/_4$ cup
250 ml	8 fl oz	1 cup
300 ml	10 fl oz ($^1/_2$ pint)	$1^1/_4$ cups
375 ml	12 fl oz	$1^1/_2$ cups
435 ml	14 fl oz	$1^3/_4$ cups
500 ml	16 fl oz	2 cups
625 ml	20 fl oz (1 pint)	$2^1/_2$ cups
750 ml	24 fl oz ($1^1/_5$ pints)	3 cups
1 litre	32 fl oz ($1^3/_5$ pints)	4 cups
1.25 litres	40 fl oz (2 pints)	5 cups
1.5 litres	48 fl oz ($2^2/_5$ pints)	6 cups
2.5 litres	80 fl oz (4 pints)	10 cups

DRY MEASURES

Metric	Imperial
30 grams	1 ounce
45 grams	1$^1/_2$ ounces
55 grams	2 ounces
70 grams	2$^1/_2$ ounces
85 grams	3 ounces
100 grams	3$^1/_2$ ounces
110 grams	4 ounces
125 grams	4$^1/_2$ ounces
140 grams	5 ounces
280 grams	10 ounces
450 grams	16 ounces (1 pound)
500 grams	1 pound, 1$^1/_2$ ounces
700 grams	1$^1/_2$ pounds
800 grams	1$^3/_4$ pounds
1 kilogram	2 pounds, 3 ounces
1.5 kilograms	3 pounds, 4$^1/_2$ ounces
2 kilograms	4 pounds, 6 ounces

LENGTH

Metric	Imperial
0.5 cm	$^1/_4$ inch
1 cm	$^1/_2$ inch
1.5 cm	$^3/_4$ inch
2.5 cm	1 inch

ABBREVIATION

tsp	teaspoon
Tbsp	tablespoon
g	gram
kg	kilogram
ml	millilitre

OVEN TEMPERATURE

	°C	°F	Gas Regulo
Very slow	120	250	1
Slow	150	300	2
Moderately slow	160	325	3
Moderate	180	350	4
Moderately hot	190/200	370/400	5/6
Hot	210/220	410/440	6/7
Very hot	230	450	8
Super hot	250/290	475/550	9/10

The recipes in this book were taken from *Tanoshii,* first published in 2013.

Photographers: Joshua Tan (Elements by the Box) and Valiant Chow

Published by Marshall Cavendish Cuisine
An imprint of Marshall Cavendish International

A member of the
Times Publishing Group

Other Marshall Cavendish Offices:
Marshall Cavendish Corporation. 99 White Plains Road, Tarrytown NY 10591-9001, USA • Marshall Cavendish International (Thailand) Co Ltd. 253 Asoke, 12th Flr, Sukhumvit 21 Road, Klongtoey Nua, Wattana, Bangkok 10110, Thailand • Marshall Cavendish (Malaysia) Sdn Bhd, Times Subang, Lot 46, Subang Hi-Tech Industrial Park, Batu Tiga, 40000 Shah Alam, Selangor Darul Ehsan, Malaysia

National Library Board, Singapore Cataloguing-in-Publication Data

Names: Yamashita, Masataka, 1960-.
Title: Get started making tea cakes & tarts / Yamashita Masataka.
Other title(s): Get started making
Description: Singapore : Marshall Cavendish Cuisine, [2017]
Identifiers: OCN 1003448934 | 978-981-47-9417-6 (hardcover)
Subjects: LCSH: Confectionery--Japan. | Cooking, Japanese. | LCGFT: Cookbooks.
Classification: DDC 641.8530952--dc23

Printed by Times Offset (M) Sdn Bhd